Store Clerks
Then and Now

Lisa Zamosky

Associate Editor
Christina Hill, M.A.

Assistant Editor
Torrey Maloof

Editorial Director
Emily R. Smith, M.A.Ed.

Project Researcher
Gillian Eve Makepeace

Editor-in-Chief
Sharon Coan, M.S.Ed.

Editorial Manager
Gisela Lee, M.A.

Creative Director
Lee Aucoin

Illustration Manager
Timothy J. Bradley

Designers
Lesley Palmer
Debora Brown
Zac Calbert
Robin Erickson

Project Consultant
Corinne Burton, M.A.Ed.

Publisher
Rachelle Cracchiolo, M.S.Ed.

Teacher Created Materials Publishing

5301 Oceanus Drive
Huntington Beach, CA 92649
http://www.tcmpub.com

ISBN 978-0-7439-9384-5

Table of Contents

Helping Customers

Store clerks help people while they shop. The people they help are called **customers** (KUHS-tuh-merz). They help customers find the things they need. Store clerks must be friendly. If they are not, customers might shop somewhere else.

⬆ Salesman helping a customer

↟ This is a store in 1914

An old cash register ➤

Much to Do

Store clerks do many things at work. They must know their stores well. Store clerks help customers find the things they need. They put price tags on items. And, they help keep the stores clean.

They also take payments for **goods**. Customers pay with money, checks, or credit cards. The money is kept in a **cash register** (REJ-uh-stir). Clerks keep track of the money. They count the money when the store opens. And, they count the money when the store closes. This way they know how much money the store has made.

▼ A modern cash register

▲ Customers shopping in a music store in Japan

◀ Cash register
drawer with
money

Rent for Less

Many stores rent items for
a fee. Most of these stores
rent movies. Have you ever
rented a movie?

▲ Clerks getting ready to open a store in China.

Training

Store clerks who work in small stores learn from other workers. Workers who know the store well teach new clerks how to do their jobs. Large stores use classes to train clerks.

This woman is ▲
training a
new clerk.

Hands-on Training

New clerks have to learn about the things they sell. Many stores train their new clerks on the products. Store clerks in candy stores might have to taste each piece of candy. Store clerks in toy stores may have to show how all the toys work. That sounds like a fun day at work!

▲ A clerk stocks shelves in a grocery store in 1939.

Filling the Shelves

Stores often bring in new items to sell. They also have to replace the items that have been bought. Store clerks place price tags on the new items. They also help to **stock** the shelves and racks. This keeps the store in order.

Bigger and Bigger

Long ago, stores were small. They had one counter and a few shelves. Stores now have many shelves full of products. The United States has over 1.6 million stock clerks! They work hard to keep the shelves stocked every day.

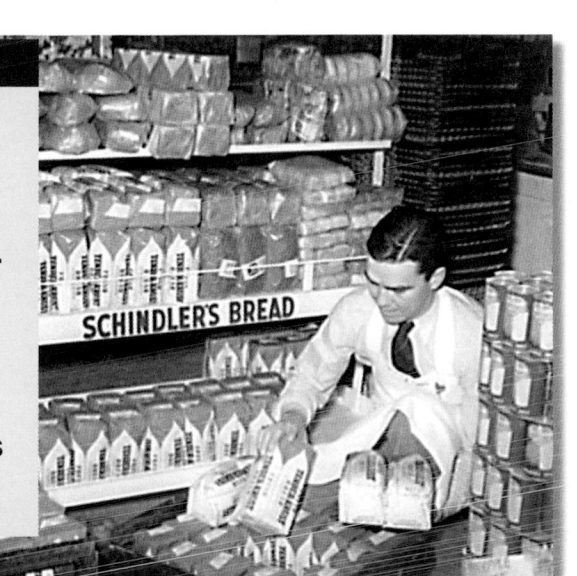

▲ Clerk stocking shelves in 1939

▲ Clerk stocking shelves today

Security

People might try to steal from stores. Today, a lot of stores have alarms. The alarm will go off if a person tries to steal. Stores also have **security** (suh-CURE-uh-tee) **guards**. They watch people in the stores. They help to keep the stores and the store clerks safe.

▲ Security guard badge

◀ Security guards walk around stores.

◀ This is a
security
camera.

Mirror, Mirror, on the Wall

Special mirrors can help keep stores safe. They are called **convex** mirrors. They are shaped like an upside-down bowl. These mirrors are placed high up on a wall. They help store clerks see an entire store.

Checking Out

Clerks must help people pay for the items they buy. They must learn to use the cash register. They need to learn to use credit card machines (muh-SHEENZ). And, they must give the customer a receipt (ruh-CEET).

Customers may return things they buy. Clerks must find out why. Is it broken? Is it the wrong size? Then, they must give the money back.

▲ Customers line up to return their items.

MOLES

Poway
Poway, CA 92064

10-29-05 12:21P 0710/0008/0768/6 1545XXX
ID# 999-8970-9487-7876-9289-9192-3114

TODDLER KNIT TO	400877687876	*	6.30	T1
KIDS SHOES	400877629012	*	13.99	T1
LIC GIRL UNDERW	045299058691	*	5.99	T1
TODDLER KNIT TO	400876980473	*	6.30	T1
TODDLER KNIT TO	400876980565	*	6.30	T1
TODDLER KNIT TO	400877687906	*	6.30	T1
TODDLER T-NECKS	400876739316	*	4.05	T1
TODDLER T-NECKS	400876739439	*	4.05	T1
TODDLER KNIT TO	400876735301	*	4.05	T1
TODDLER KNIT TO	400876735394	*	4.05	T1

	SUBTOTAL		61.38
T1=	61.38 @ 7.750% TAX		4.76
	TOTAL		66.14

MASTERCARD   XXXXXXXXXXXX   66.14
APPROVED   029641

NOW HIRING FOR THE HOLIDAY SEASON.
FLEXIBLE SCHEDULING
IMMEDIATE ASSOCIATE DISCOUNT. APPLY TODAY!

cheap shoes
CARMEL MOUNTAIN PLAZA

SAN DIEGO, CA 92128-4641

0261734 SF TOD BLK LTHR	$12.99	T
29542030 PLU T PINK/BLUE	$3.99	T
Original Price $7.99		
Promo 5 - Pink BO -$4.00		
	$16.98	
SubTotal	$1.31	
Tax 7.75%	$18.29	
TOTAL	$18.29	

MasterCard
Card #:   XXXXXXXXXXXX
Auth #:   029623

10/29/05
1:15:04 PM

4506-1302-53767
Transaction By: 4506

◆ Customers receive receipts that list everything they bought.

◆ Samples of receipts

15

▲ Stores stay open extra hours during the holiday season.

Working Hours

Store hours can vary. There are stores that are open 24 hours a day! This gives people more time to shop. Holidays are busy for store clerks. A lot of people shop during this time. So, stores may stay open longer.

Most stores have **sales** during the holidays. This is a great way to get people to choose their stores. Big sales may last a whole week. Store clerks must know about all of the sales. They have to answer people's questions.

Winter Gifts

Nine out of the ten busiest shopping days are in December.

⬆ Sales are a good way to get people into stores.

Retail Stores

There are different kinds of **retail stores**. There are drug stores where people can get medicine (MED-uh-sin). There are large stores that sell everything from food to car parts. And, there are stores that just sell clothes or toys. Each store clerk knows the best way to sell the things in his or her store.

◄ A clerk rings up purchases on his cash register.

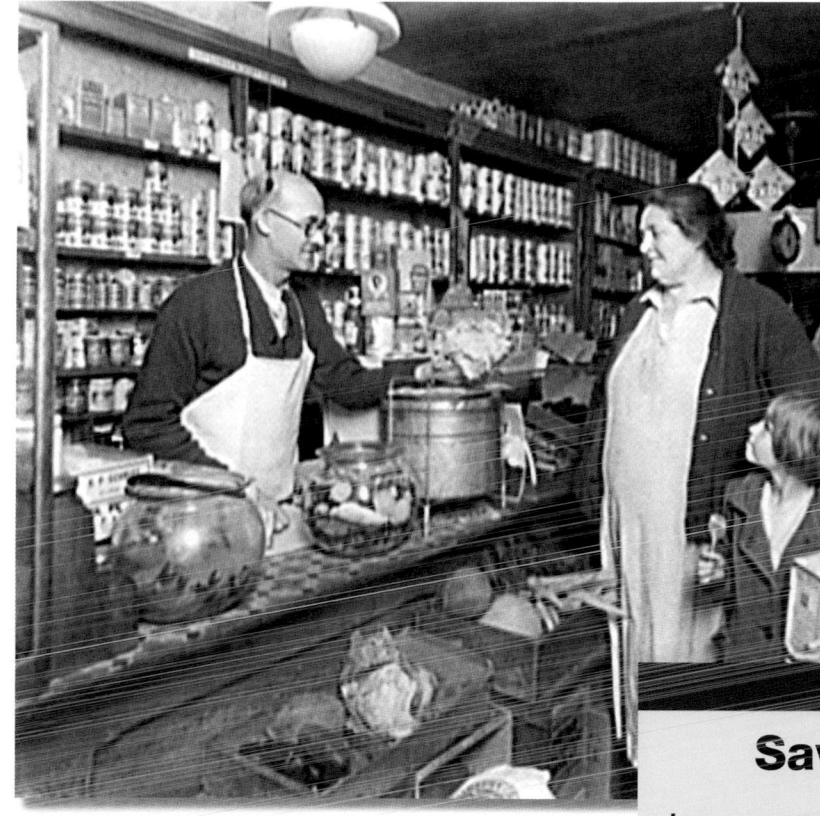

⬆ This is a grocery store in the early 1900s.

Saving Time

Long ago, there were no malls. There were no big department stores. Stores were small and only sold certain items. People would have to walk across town to get from store to store. Now, people can drive to one big mall. There, they have lots of stores to choose from.

⬅ Shopping malls have many types of stores.

Stores and More

Today, stores can be very big. Store clerks may work in just a small part of a large store. Malls have many kinds of stores. And, some malls have more than just stores. Some malls have water parks. Others have movie theaters (THEE-uh-tuhrz). Some even have hotels and golf courses!

▼ This mall has an ice-skating rink.

↟ The Mall of America is so large that it has its own amusement park.

Big Size Shopping

The Mall of America is the largest mall in the United States. It has more than 500 stores. It also has tons of places to eat and things to see. It is big enough to fit seven baseball stadiums (STAY-dee-uhmz) inside!

Being a Store Clerk

Store clerks help customers find the things they need. Good store clerks can make it easier to shop. They can also make shopping more fun. Stores like to hire friendly people to work as clerks. This can help a store be **successful** (suhk-SES-ful).

Clerks ➤ work hard to help customers.

▲ This store clerk sells fruits and vegetables.

Store clerks have exciting jobs. They meet new people every day. It is a good job for people who like to work with others.

A Day in the Life Then

Abraham Lincoln
(1809–1865)

Many people remember Abraham Lincoln because he was the president. But, he had many jobs before he was president. He once was a store clerk. He worked in the store during the day. He slept in the store at night. He was paid $15 a month. He worked hard and saved his money. Then, he bought his own general store.

Let's pretend to ask Abraham Lincoln some questions about his job.

Why did you decide to be a store clerk?

I did not have much money when I was young. This job gives me money and a place to live. I did not have a lot of job experience. But, I learned quickly.

What is your day like?

I have to stock the shelves when new items come. I sweep the floors. I make sure that the store is clean. Then, I wait to help customers. When I have free time, I like to read.

What do you like most about your job?

I love meeting new people. Many people come to the store and tell me jokes and stories. It is a lot of fun.

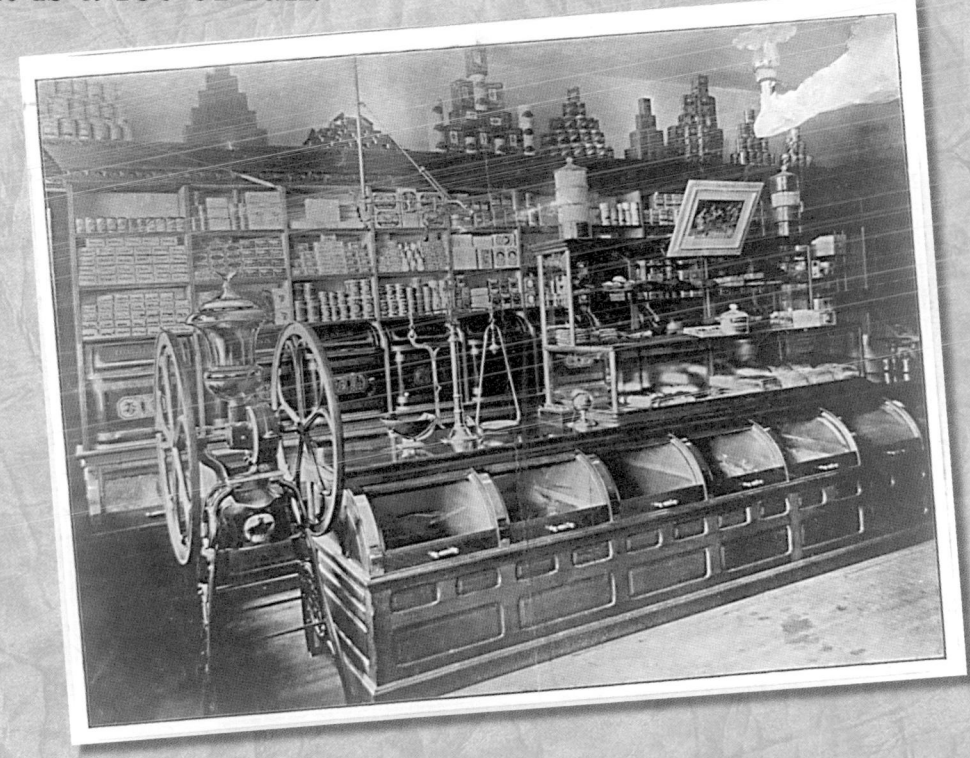

▲ This store looks a lot like the store Mr. Lincoln worked in as a store clerk.

Tools of the Trade Then

◀ Store clerks used cash registers that looked like this. They were used only for paper money and coins.

Store clerks had to keep the stores clean. They swept the floor often. ▶

◀ Shelves were important tools for store clerks. They kept the stores clean and organized.

▲ Price tags were tied to items. The store clerk wrote each price on a tag.

Tools of the Trade Now

◀ New cash registers look like this one. They have credit card machines. Customers today do not have to have paper money to shop.

Stores still use shelves to store items. Ladders and **forklifts** may be used to reach high items. ▶

◀ Today, clerks don't have to type out the price of an item. They just scan the **barcode**.

A Day in the Life Now

Harmony Deimling

Harmony Deimling is a store clerk. She works at a grocery store. She stocks shelves with food and supplies. She also helps customers. In her free time she likes to paint and draw.

Why did you decide to become a store clerk?

My mother was a store clerk. She loved it. I always admired and looked up to her. So, I decided to become a store clerk, too. It is a great job. I go to work early in the morning. After work, I go to college.

What is your day like?

In the morning I stock the shelves. I also make sure that the store is clean. Then, I help bag groceries. Some people need my help to put what they buy in their cars. It can be hard work. But, I really enjoy it.

⬆ Ms. Deimling works in a grocery store like this one.

What do you like most about your job?

I like meeting new people. But, I also like the friendships I have made with our regular customers. These are people that always shop at our store. They make my job fun!

Glossary

barcode—a set of lines that can be scanned for information

cash register—a machine that adds the amount of sales, and has a drawer in which cash can be kept

convex—a curved circle or sphere

customers—people who buys things

forklifts—machines that can lift and lower large items

goods—things bought and sold

receipt—a piece of paper that shows the names and prices of the goods purchased

retail stores—stores that sell items to the public

sales—selling goods at lower prices

security guards—people who work to keep stores

Index

Credits

Acknowledgements

Special thanks to Harmony Deimling for providing the *Day in the Life Now* interview. Ms. Deimling is a store clerk in Huntington Beach, California.

Image Credits

front cover Comstock; p.1 Comstock; p.4 Photos.com; p.5 (top) Denver Public Library; p.5 (bottom) Hemera Technologies, Inc; p.6 (top) Jostein Hauge/ Shutterstock, Inc.; p.6 (bottom) Christy Thompson/Shutterstock, Inc.; p.7 (top) Hemera Technologies, Inc.; p.7 (bottom) Photos.com; p.8 China Photos/Getty Images; p.9 (top) Tim Boyle/Getty Images; p.9 (bottom) Krzysztof Nieciecki/ Shutterstock, Inc.; p.10 The Library of Congress; p.11 (top) The Library of Congress; p.11 (bottom) Tim Boyle/Getty Images; p.12 (left) Francis Miller/ Stringer/Getty Images; p. 12 (right) photos.com; p. 13 (top) Michael Mauney/ Getty Images; p.13 (bottom) Ginae/BigStock.com, Inc.; p.14 Tim Boyle/Getty Images; p.15 (top) Chris Hondros; p.15 (bottom) Emily Smith; p.16 (top) Dan Callister/Newsmakers/Getty Images; p.16 (bottom) Photos.com; p.17 Spencer Platt/Getty Images; p.18 Scott Olson/Getty Images; p.19 (top) The Library of Congress; p.19 (bottom) Photos.com; p.20 Taolmor/Shutterstock, Inc.; p.21 Karen Bleier/AFP/Getty Images; p.22 Michael L. Abramson/Getty Images; p.23 (top) Jim Lopes/Shutterstock, Inc.; p.23 (bottom) Clipart.com; p.24 The Library of Congress; p.25 The Library of Congress; p.26 (top) Christophe Testi/Shutterstock, Inc.; p.26 (bottom right) Catherine Auvil/Shutterstock, Inc.; p.26 (middle) The Library of Congress; p.26 (bottom left) The Library of Congress; p.27 (bottom left) Stuart Elflett/Shutterstock, Inc.; p.27 (middle) Loannis Loannou/ Shutterstock, Inc.; p.27 (bottom right) Krzysztof Nieciecki/Shutterstock, Inc.; p.27 (middle) Roman Milert/Shutterstock, Inc.; p.28 Courtesy of Christina Hill; p.29 Andriy Rovenko/Shutterstock, Inc.; back cover The Library of Congress